# A CHILD OF STORM

## A CHILD OF STORM
### ACKNOWLEDGEMENTS

'Tesla Talks to Time' and 'Tesla and Edison Argue' were published by *Treehouse*.

'Samuel Clemens', 'War of Currents', and 'Faraday Cage 1, 2, 6' were published by *Lime Hawk*.

'Stealing Tesla's Thunder' and 'Tesla's Manifesto' were published by *Luna Luna*.

'Eastern Hop Hornbeam' was published by *IDK Magazine*.

'Rhododendron' was published by *The Laurel Review*.

'Flowering Dogwood' was published by *Lungfull*.

'Geometry of Cascading Rooms' was published by *Pax Americana*.

'Tesla is Born', 'Optica', 'Edwin Davis & The Electric Chair', and 'Topsy' were published by *Sensitive Skin*.

# A CHILD OF STORM
## POEMS BY MICHAEL J. WILSON

STALKING HORSE PRESS
SANTE FE, NEW MEXICO

**A CHILD OF STORM**

Copyright © 2016 by Michael J. Wilson
ISBN: 978-0-9970629-3-9
Library of Congress Control Number: 2016943993

First paperback edition published by Stalking Horse Press, October 2016

All rights reserved. Except for brief passages quoted for review or academic purposes, no part of this book may be reproduced, stored in a retrieval system, or transmitted by any means without the written permission of the author and publisher. Published in the United States by Stalking Horse Press.

www.stalkinghorsepress.com

Design by James Reich

Stalking Horse Press
Santa Fe, New Mexico

Stalking Horse Press requests that authors designate a nonprofit, charitable, or humanitarian organization to receive a portion of revenue from the sales of each title. Michael J. Wilson has chosen the Transgender Resource Center of New Mexico.

## CONTENTS

History Lessons: Houston Street - 9
Tesla Is Born - 11
Facts - 12
Tesla's Father - 13
Tesla and Edison Argue - 14
Optica - 15
Tesla's Father - 16
Tesla Responds - 17
Tesla's Manifesto - 18
We Are Men Endlessly - 19
William Kemmler & The Electric Chair - 20
Edwin Davis & The Electric Chair - 21
On Harold Pitney Brown - 22
Topsy - 23
War of Currents - 24
Tesla's Father - 27
Samuel Clemens - 28
Fragments of Olympian Gossip - 29
Tesla Writes an Obituary - 30
Tesla's Father - 31
Tesla Talks to Time - 32
History Lessons: The Rock Dove - 35
Faraday Cage - 37
American Plum - 43
One Strand A Mile Long - 44
Study (Sand Dune and Tree) - 45
Eastern Hop Hornbeam - 48
Cherry Birch - 49

Eastern Red Cedar - 50
Pitch Pine - 51
Eastern Redbud - 52
Boxing Day - 53
Challenger Carried - 54
Red Oak - 55
Rhododendron - 56
Study (Three Seasons) - 57
Highbush Bluberry - 63
History Lessons: Santa Fe - 64
Elimination - 66
A Joke - 68
American Chestnut - 69
Love Poem - 70
Flowering Dogwood - 71
Pecan - 72
Buckeye - 73
Anima - 74
American Elm - 75
Black Locust - 76
Lungfish - 77
Study (Balloon Boy) - 78
Yellow Birch - 82
Cranberry - 83
Geometry of Cascading Rooms - 84
Ristra - 85
History Lessons: Ground Zero - 88

*To my parents:*
*Who never minded that I wanted to spend my life chasing lightning.*

## HISTORY LESSONS : HOUSTON STREET

It's fall, we are standing on Houston at the corner of Broadway looking west you want coffee and can't remember where Starbucks is but do remember where Balthazaar is and Prada and Ben Sherman.

The buildings are covered in ads, towering, half-naked people selling watches and perfume. Houston has always sold. SoHo has the largest collection of iron-faced buildings in the world. The sun blinds. I only smell steam garbage skin.

I want to explain my distances and want to know yours. Down there somewhere Tesla experimented with x-rays and radio waves until the fire took everything. These streets are canyons, rivers, everything is flat. I feel claustrophobic.

The sky is pale. Everything washing to the sea. If we walk down Houston we will find a coffee shop where Tesla's lab was. Across the street a vacant lot and a movie theater.

Tell me what sort of solution there is.
The Starbucks is your distance.
The vacant lot is mine.

You are impatient.
You are tired of my obsession with lights.
You want things to be solid, never wavering.
But this is a city that constantly wavers. It is a mutable object on an island in a delta in a new country on a planet full of forces

moving constantly. You know that Tesla left for the west after this city beat him down.

You want to see ground zero. I turn away when we take the R through Cortlandt. There are holes in the walls that look into vacant light. It is like seeing a person on life support. The world is not black and white. It is a swirl of radiation green.

We are poles in a field standing against whatever weather comes, not sure that we can take it, but standing. And you want your coffee. I see in your eyes that you want to go inside Crate & Barrel and then to Uni Qlo. There's a sale on cashmere.

I want to walk across the Brooklyn Bridge and smell the salt air sweeping over me and watch the sun set across the Statue of Liberty. You want to meet your parents at ground zero and watch. I am reminded that Tesla was also beaten in the west.

## TESLA IS BORN

The sound of a shell at your ear
        in an expansive void
                that is the mouth of the universe
Lightening across the curve of the eye
        A crack in the spheres
                allowing a peek at the undergarments of God
And then the earth is revealed
        by the pounding of rain
                knives     broken bones
What is this moment
        where the sky pulls itself apart at the sutures
                drops a child
                        on the waiting flower
                        of Croatia

## FACTS

His eyes were gray –
        the reflection in them water – when he was born
lightning spun in the valley – his mother's womb
        contracted with the roll of thunder –

He was 6'2" and 142 lbs –
        he never fluctuated – had OCD
the door would lock unlock lock unlock lock unlock lock
        but the window would stand open –

His vision was plagued with flashes of light –
        thoughts were solid objects mirrored in dream –
patent filings–death rays–coils hugging magnets until they glowed
        His body a tower that drilled into the earth –

He believed sex would diminish him –
        evacuate cells of their potency – his brain
was so strong that it drained the color from his eyes for fuel
        He believed that pigeons were the souls of the unborn –

At the top of the world he would sit in darkness – would count
        the radii of every single bird –

## TESLA'S FATHER

On his deathbed – all of us – on his deathbed – Dane
      opened his eyes – after daysweeksmonths

You had said it was from a horse – from a fall – from a height

He opened his eyes – Nikola – they were slits of light
in that darkness unimaginable – dim but
looking like the sun in that
                pitch
                        black
                              room

Dane raised his hand his finger
      unfolding like the end of a fern – fiddled – plucked
his voice – trembling violin – opening in that chamber

All of us in that coffin together and he
      said your name – the word *pushed* – and

      the light went out of the sun

## TESLA AND EDISON ARGUE

50,000,    sir        ,

for the redesign     ,    the improvement    ,    the

generator    *I* fixed   ,   sir,

One year   , I waited      ,

18 per week  ,        sir , I would

have to work 53 years      ,    give

me 25 ,      I have earned 25 ,    sir   ,

*Tesla  ,*

      *you don't understand our American humor  ,*

## OPTICA

       What does
       a glass of light look like?

Mercury
      meniscus – blue-hinged
casting
laziness on your hand

       What is its taste?

Oddly lemon
      rose – juniper

      gin cleaning fluid
           static

It flows uphill

      seeps

in the opposite of shadow

This flask of it – corked at the hip

recedes into memory
the second you've seen it

## TESLA'S FATHER

You – climbing THAT mount
        to pretend you could hold THAT fire –

It is un un un un un

I see you blinded by the very idea of light
        Building a cage for God's breath
            !

At night when you sleep
        the billion lidless eyes of the sky open
        like God's ice in winter –
            like the soul in hell's fire –

HE will end your efforts – I fear
        in firelight death

Knowing you turn your back on GLORY –
        I die twice
            !

## TESLA RESPONDS

When I first saw a river move
        I could see the transmission from A - B

Father – I am St. Theresa mid-ecstasy
            Science – the arrow of God – in my chest

## TESLA'S MANIFESTO

The earth is a workable solution

Take this glass bulb        plant it
      watch stars be shamed to silence

We can till fields until we grow old – grow illumination
like fodder for cows – cities

People the universe and –

crack
      every goddamn star
                    until
we find hollow caverns of diamonds

Until we make them sing with *our* radiance

## WE ARE MEN ENDLESSLY

The earth covered in small crackling silver globes – The earth without lines – without wire – outlets – The freedom of being never with out…

*The earth is a conductor – The atmosphere a conductor – There is a stratum between the conducting atmosphere and the conducting earth – an insulator…*

Here a building in New York City – The generator inside spins in its casings free with no one to stop it…

*What is the capacity of earth – What charge does it contain – It must have a charge – All processes of mechanical separation have charge…*

That power surge lifts then points your head towards sky – A light is coming from out there – It is hitting your eye…

*Is this static or kinetic – If kinetic then it is a question of time – When men will succeed in attaching machinery to the very wheelwork of nature…*

Imagine earth covered in man – The sky will dark then light – Here is that Colorado that New York City filling at last with what we can make…

*A single ray of light from a distant star falling upon the eye of a tyrant – May have altered the course – May have changed destiny – May have transformed the surface of the globe…*

We are men – endlessly –

*So intricate – So inconceivably complex…*

# WILLIAM KEMMLER & THE ELECTRIC CHAIR

A chair
                      wooden
                    polished to glowing

       it could be at any table
in any home in any America

It's insidious – how simple – how
           normal

If death is so easy –
                death is *always* easy – but

        something *too* safe about a chair


When I took that hatchet and
when that hatchet met Tillie's head – was it
              this clean
          polished
       about to eat a bowl of cereal –


The room is watching

It wants a reaction
                give something
                            they did so much

           this moment
      deserves a reaction:


*I wish you all luck with this*

## EDWIN DAVIS & THE ELECTRIC CHAIR

Brown came with a crate.
        The kind milk bottles condense in.

He sat it down. In the center of the room.
        I had spent the day clearing cobwebs, a rug.

I used parts of the crate to make the chair.

Stringing the wires, using the Edison diagram
        The Brown instructions.

I shot 1000 volts through Kemmler
        then again until he burst to flame.

The skin around the metal became leather.
        *They would have done better using an axe.*

I shot volts into a woman. Into the man who shot McKinley.

I got to meet J.P. Morgan. Twice.

        Every time –
The smell –

## ON HAROLD PITNEY BROWN

What circus is America?

We raised a tent in Chicago and the coils
radiated cool from the center out – they
        performed – were magic

A sundial of progress

In New Jersey they go about collecting dogs
paying children to gather them – a penny a pooch
        three in a row 300 volts
           baking their insides for what –

He has them convinced I am a charlatan
Man is not ready –

I tear the tent
        throw coil to the sea

Perhaps the kraken wants to end its permanent night

## TOPSY

                flesh is stone –
      rippling –
      will not be caged –

the neck – frozen
        at an angle – some degrees
off normal –

the man smiling broadly
his hand on the polished wood handle
of a switch

                – the crowd is not breathing
            – the children are staring

                  wires from the switch
            to a frame around the head
            to shackles on the ankles –

      the elephant – begins – to bleed – from its ears

      poisoned strangled electrocuted

            she falls –

you cannot imagine – the amount of heaving skin

        she refused to cross to death
        wired where she stood – they had to bring death to her

the earthquake of trumpets –

# WAR OF CURRENTS

## 60 HZ

      Stars are just stars –

    At night         walking the dog

The one over that tree cycles red
then white
        then red – it is a code – some orbiting Alien hardware speaking across millennia

    The mood smears a Milky Way across the sky

    It hides behind the clacking branches
        it kindles

## SKIN EFFECT

    January:

The other night in bed the universe explained itself

The expanding

How objects are moving apart like a dissecting
        crowd post-flashmob

The voice of the universe is hide tensed over drum

The echo that is a voice in a chat room:

> *Edison invented the lightbulb*
> *just so he could throw shade at Tesla*

## 12 V

And history will be kind to no one

## TRANSFORMER

      A hand at the thigh – in the photo
Mark Twain is embracing light – Tesla is a cypher
a broken limb torn from a pine tree

He believed sexuality was a drain – touching the
void of aura

In college – running in heavy monsoon there is a figure under the roof of the Palace of the Governors – in the flash between drops it is R is face in hands is knees on forehead –
      And then he will vanish    will never come back – will have become the broken filament in the bulb of 2002 – then flashes of contact – snapshots of his refusing to be hugged –
      His mother will call – will break the silence of glass and explain the universe within him was a fragile terrarium – that no outside thing could touch – that he feared the contamination of this self – that contact sucked him dry –

                                Body locked forever in a
dark room on a coast that is never near and never far –

                         And you will sympathize with retreat to
penthouses full of pigeons and you will want to stop running

   I am unable to explain it – you will – and yet you will not

## TESLA'S FATHER

The pile of letters – yellowed string around their waists
    each professing your over-worked nature – your
        inability to rest

That year you were dead – when we thought the waters
    had taken you – the murmuring between us
        dried to a bone-filled gully

That year I held the letters – prayed to the fireplace
    searched the heavens for signs from God
        that you were only hiding yourself from the light

All this time – within the letters of your life
    the bones of breaking down were corseted

When you were back – miracle that it was – you were changed

    I hold your hand while you sleep – you sweat
    through the night – insecurity pouring

## SAMUEL CLEMENS

He stares into the light suspended between his fingers
       – the glory of invention –

The phantasm flickers     it
       breathes     the respirations illuminate his face

          It is an anemone from
    the pool from which life itself crawled

Tesla
      in the darkness beyond revelation
                  his body slashed in glare

        watches Clemens watch
the moment God was done and man took over

## FRAGMENTS OF OLYMPIAN GOSSIP

JP's nose is a mass of red tissue without a single sense to its credit

That tower of Tesla's shoots electricity, he thinks he can split the world in half

IN BOLDNESS OF CONCEPTION

March is bad for investors

There is a sense that JP and Westinghouse wanted Tesla to succeed only so Edison would not

IN GREATNESS

A ray gun, an earth splitter, wireless electricity, the perpetual motion generator, the fire of Olympus handed to man and allowed to light their puny caves

JP's nose was the color of a plum, it looked like plastic, it swallowed his face

AND IN USEFULNESS TO MANKIND

Everything Tesla made, he destroyed

## TESLA WRITES AN OBITUARY

I left you New York –

Walked the mountain paths of Colorado – found
        a field to plant my bulbs

I'm the tired circus sidekick – arms spread – tied to a wheel
        waiting for daggers

The clear dark night steamed with Milky Way and nothing

Here is some patent for a ray gun on a receipt for a hat
        now – let me spill anonymous electrons in peace

You have your direct currents to the ears of America

I am not inclined to be king
        Quietly – I will build a city of light
            capture the sun
drive my fists into the ground until I split the earth in two

I will walk into the sky –

Edison,       you have no hobby –
      care for no amusement –
      disregard the rules of hygiene –
you have

immense   blind   contempt     for learning
      knowledge
           decency

trusting only good    American   sense –

Leave me in my empty with Clemens

Forget you ever knew a Nikola Tesla

## TESLA'S FATHER

But–the church *is* a laboratory–the greatest experiment conceived
    Think about the hinge of the continent–the range of
        Alps – the crack
            of deus ex rock against deus ex rock

The eyes of God are fire – water – are land with no horizon –
    God's eyes are not eyes – they are black holes eating –
        The hands of the sun turn the cog of the earth

and the cog twists until red – until it burns the silt of wanting

In that fever – what universe birthed from your toil
    The heat of my memory sears the open wound of life –
        You will die alone in a tower of feathers – a Babel of
            bullshit

Nikola – what good have you found in your fields afire ?

## TESLA TALKS TO TIME

The world was at war I spiraled energy weapons in dark hotel rooms lined with aluminum foil and patent applications – sleeping with pigeons at the top of New York I am dead and this darkness is a rolling black field

Maybe the universe is direct
                              I alternate on this

I put on my quilt and sit on a bench in the park from my pockets I pull the confetti of long ago filings I decide that this is the way to the center of the earth

To remember Houston Street and the wireless universe that could be –

The colors were fantastic I shot through with full spectrums I was brought to my knees brimming on the might of the river of progress on the fire within everything – there is a positive and negative polarity in my stomach – it nots and un-nots

Do you remember when my father thought me dead was dead did die then did not die was alive has this even happened yet – it happens now –

My father stands at the foot of my bed he is ridiculous in his priestly attire he has an elephant's foot in his hands it has been hollowed and filled with umbrellas he is mouthing a word over and over and that word is Dane the word is dead the word is broken into a pile of stone

– Did you kill your brother was there even a horse to fall from was the sun at an angle where it shot rings into your eyes as you did it was the river the color of your eyes –

The pigeons are steel-colored and mechanical in their roosts of hotel drawers and hotel bathtub

What of Oppenheimer's splitting?

Einstein warned us while gleefully filling in the blanks writing equations on a chalkboard in Roosevelt's office – they would never ask me I suppose I don't know a damn thing about bombs – they are not building one in the not desert of the not quite west –

Clemens told me to be careful

I wanted to break everything did break everything look at this pile of broken things

Standing in his Twain coat holding that ball of fire it became some metaphor for the history of the world between his fingers spinning in that darkness – a Mark spinning a Twain

I look like a golem in that picture – all void – all imagined body floating in immense space

Everything got faster will the future be even more so?

Lightning is hummingbirds bees moths in a glass jar beating

against the walls until everything burns in terrible illumination – the glass won't melt but will bow

We climb mountains we steal fires we pick which piece of wood made which lick of flame and in the process the fire is put out

When Edison died I walked into the darkness around me and pulled the globe of glass from inside myself and I struck it into the earth – hard fast and it caught itself on the rocks it began to glow or I thought it did then the shattering glass expanded in all directions and everything seemed like reflection until the field was stars until the field was a grid expanding faster than the speed of vision –

We may all be geniuses but then we also must be fools

# HISTORY LESSONS : THE ROCK DOVE

My arms outstretch and my 8-year-old frame becomes covered with birds. Three on one arm inspect the stripes on my shirt, two on the other check the seams. There is one on my head supervising.

If they wanted they could lift me take me to the furthest reaches of the world. Away from this square, this city. Away from the planet, some little prince of the 1980s.

Adaptation is the process where an organism becomes able to live in its habitat or habitats easier. An 8-year-old child is taken into space by a small group of pigeons. He slowly becomes able to live in the limited environment.

The pigeon originates in Europe, northern Africa and southern Asia but is found in nearly every city in the world. One of the first animals to be domesticated, pigeons seen today are feral ancestors of birds raised for food, work, or as pets.

This one at my feet in this square in Bath is grey with black bands on its wings and tail. Its head is a soft darker shade with an oil slick purple and green shine. This is a pure bred. They have striking orange eyes and pinkish feet.

It's right foot is broken. Hanging by a thread. It hobbles, adding to its already odd walk. Birds can't wince. Its brow doesn't furrow. Toes hang limply, it walks on the spurs of its feet.

This is 15 years after I was possibly taken. I'm sitting at a café staring at the entrance of the roman baths. I am tossing crumbs of bread to this broken bird. I am so firmly grounded.

The baths were started in 60AD. The pigeon had already been domestic for 10,000 years. The Egyptians, the Romans, they carried messages in every war until the 1940s.

They are adaptable because they naturally live on cliff faces. They lay their eggs on bare surfaces with a minimal layer of nest. In Trafalgar, in 2003 feeding the birds was banned. In 2007 the ban extended out of the square wrapping the city in less and less.

There are few birds in the square today. Definitely not enough to carry children or imaginations. This broken bird in bath hobbles across the square to the church. It sits in the grass. Not made for rock faces anymore. But nesting still.

# FARADAY CAGE

### I

The locking of the door

Three. Times. The. Locking.

Safety in that
        quiet
        encased self in that


At night the sound of people out on the street causes panic –
    dreams of invasion – hands always hands

scratching at the window
        reaching from the walls

Eyeless face in the darkness
      where do the face's tears go –

        A realization

        They are here to take everything
        pots        pans
            televisions

        the reflection in your eye


The memory of that reflection

## 2

In the bathroom there is a Jewish prayer mistaken for Elvish

I wash my face          pools of clear cool water
       poured over cheeks        red with heat with rash

Then stare at the eyes staring at the eyes staring at the eyes

Towel to face     gentle    eyes to mirror to mirror to

      one twisting serrated leg
      stuck on my chin       it moves

More on hands    in the sink    eight twitching yellow limbs

## 3

Outside the Roman baths pigeons wait for crumbs

The sandwich is baguette with butter a thin slice of ham
some orange cheese

Pigeons inelegant in their oil slick feathers

Here is one walking on the side of its foot
the anklebone jutting out the side a dowel burried in Play-Doh

Toes are permanently clenched and these shoes are too tight

Inside the baths the water is the color of oxidized copper
smell of sulfur and desert rain triggers memories of monsoons

Heat emanates

The broken pigeon looks at the sandwich
        bobs its head once

# 4

a field of static     growing like wheat     corn    soy    the little sprouts – curling fiddle-head ferns – unpacking     becoming television signals in the night air
        a row of light-bulbs with snapped filaments and
        clouded glass
some of the kids were talking about that place      they called it haunted – the strange monolithic house – red brick melting into the hills              some     not all
        of the older people mention a field lit up at night –
stealing the electricity from the town – grass humming songs
        over the fields
the man there – not now – then
        was a vampire     wraith        tall inky night in
a coat    his hands were long       his eyes were a horse's –
        pools of deep brown oil
he claimed he had a laser a ray gun a drill to split the world in half and he locked himself up there maybe died up there
        maybe he never died –
they embed wire mesh in their walls       it's the only way to not hear the screams

# 5

At night the windows are open – the cat
stares into the darkness beyond the doorframe

    And I know there are coyotes

but the door stands open – air moves slowly in
out of the space – barely cooling barely worth the effort

Imagine a bird on the ledge – thinking about coming in
about plucking itself – escaping the nightmare of roost

That hesitancy they always carry – they move like film
    skipping

    Doves are vessels of unborn souls

        Coyotes contain the chaos of the world in their eyes
        but also the calm at the center of the chaos

With the light on in the kitchen – I sleep – unsound
                      unsound
            the cat watches the door
                    does not sleep

## 6

When they went to pick the new Pope
they built a room-sized Faraday Cage
>to prevent eavesdropping – leaks – I suppose there
are those who would leak that room of talking

I unspool the mesh – like wrapping paper

Cover the inside of the walls of the bedroom we used to share

It glistens – mica – quartz – fractals of light on fractals of adobe

I static myself in the center
knowing full well I have crossed the threshold of sane

There will be no phones – computers –
>I write notes on torn Kleenex – roll them into canes
and float them into the darkness beyond the
windows

May they wash on some shore – be found by birds or tarantulas
>unreadable – but useful – everything
nests eventually

May the echo that is my ghost skip on your page like a frame
>of film melting

## AMERICAN PLUM

Huron –

      bury your seeds –

            soften them up –

## ONE STRAND A MILE LONG

Small wormy thing – housed
in a cabinet – a drawer – a nest of straw

This un-forming begins with hands – soft – or not
gently picking up the package of cocoon

The whiteness of peeling – of un-doing
it is a blankness – erasure – rapture

What does the silk worm think as its life is unraveled
fifty thousand for one length –

In the broader sense – what does one death matter
one here – one thousand

A sniper picking each off from the safety of the rooftops
we will never see the whites of these eyes

And maybe these deaths are unimportant

Milky strands form from eyes nose mouth
insides pressing like through a sieve –

The barriers of the room are not so pointed
that they stand by themselves

## STUDY (SAND DUNE AND TREE)

Plants buried in the Sahara grow through the airless dark

Albino cave salamanders reach unseeing hands toward light

These flagellant trees
        arms raised mid-cat o' nine prayer

Blast bark into sand
        miniature – black – itching your neck


        Roots – blood vessel cages that echo in your organs

Vessels branch infinitely smaller smaller smaller…

They will continue out of your body
        to the floor
        they will root you in place

Imagine the insides of an eyelid

    : now :

Close your eyes and stare into the sun
        this –
                the color of the great universal start button

        A sky – always blue – against red O'Keefe dunes

She designed frames that pulled her paintings from the wall

        Eventually

        she tired of framing

Entire rooms have been lost in her paintings

        Roots melt into rock bending toward pockets of water

Underfoot – this tuft of grey/blue sage

The roots make miles to the water-filled arroyo

This six-inch flat bristle-plant goes 0-60
        Icarus : falling

The stems tread darkness to attempt light

My fingers twitch – full of ink
        dip a scabbed quill to my thumb
        you can trace whom it has touched
        what it smelled of – when

To move you must pour talc over everything –

A soul up-roots it sucks oxygen from trees and lunges into the
        desert

Sand oceans – two-hundred feet of gravity pushing
this tree will be buried alive

Will it keep growing on conserved light held in its branches
        leaves transparent ghosts

Or once the wave moves on
        will it all be paper cut-out negative leaves

Though Icarus isn't right for this poem
        no one flies
                hubris is not the moral : something like a
pressing a drying out a locking it all down ... this is ...

        Sisyphus :

                constant – hope – grasping

Taking off color placing paint in tubes unwrapping taut
        skin-like canvases

This is what I am doing

If you breathe in red sand
        seeds will grow unchecked : wind around through
        every damn pore to whatever light they may need

        : you know they will :

Stare at the sky eyes closed
        this is the red I am talking about

The same that plants in sand grow to

If you breathe this red

        your network of veins : burning lace that they are

        will rupture : like light under sand

            will pull themselves up

                toward water.

## EASTERN HOP HORNBEAM

Here a shore glass-draped in the blue leaves of buildings
Inside – a black noiselessness – a clearing –

Want to stack moments like a necklace like the scales of hops
like a spine this Eastern Hornbeam – bone-ish and slow – seeing
a history

Want to see what this continent has to offer – but this universe
is full of reflective towers and Leonard Cohen songs

>   Imagine lower Manhattan as bare as a glacier –

>   :

>   I will wait for you to clear the ground

>   Wait for you to ease your hesitation

>   Of being responsible –

>   :

>   Then re-wood –

Imagine it too thick to enter – almost – the devil is in the
    details
an oyster tonguing a secret pearl

I hang my dark America on the thought of that moment

>   the first tree felled – the terrible unveiling of fresh
>   skin –

## CHERRY BIRCH

You tell me to chew a birch twig and it tastes like wintergreen and I'm shocked by the numbing : that wooden thing in my mouth – Even in December I can tell that you are hot under your clothes that you have the itch to get naked : I won't stop you there is an empty spot on the desk : fold them there : Sheets are hissing :

## EASTERN RED CEDAR

You
        smell
                like
                cedar berries     and sawdust
                        mixed with plastic

You say: The radiator is full of steam

It's closed system
probably full of some black death
we wouldn't want to know about :

Remember when we had a stove in the kitchen
the grass comes yellow squared where the woodpile is
remembered

How
        did
                this sweater get a hole in it

How does a moth get passed all that smell

You mumble
Something about an old dog you used to know
        a cold snowy day
                a fall by the woods
                        when you were ten
The radiator punches the air and you look
at the discolored circle on the floor where the stove was

You say these things only comfort on the first cold day

That slipped stitches in sweaters only get bigger

## PITCH PINE

There was fire in the caldera

I walked the long stretch that we walked :

   When we used to do things the valley was open forested and the caldera wasn't bulging from the stress of pressing underneath :

      Today the path – muddy – black – trees stinking of caramel everything sugar passed hard crack :

         Halfway to the rock we sat on ate our lunches on a charred cone had sealed itself to protect the seeds blocks all paths :

           It sits on the windowsill in the kitchen where the mixer I bought you sits in its box and I can't bring myself to throw out that last unopened yogurt :

           It smells like charcoal
          wet earth
                    sheets after a fevered night's sleep :

                I waited for the unlock : I imagined getting a hammer :

## EASTERN REDBUD

I drive into the woods & stop at some random spot : I drive up the mountain & stop at some random spot & walk into the tree-line : I get out & walk to a random spot in the tree-line & go until a fallen tree : I find a fallen tree & sit down :

Down the path ahead slender branches bead red : slender branches that Judas hung from & how does that become a part of the whole : pools of red absorb into ground collect then vanish :

The vanishing is the situation I desire : the woods a shield the car pathway : I stare into the rows of aspen that silently rock on their feet : I count the beads of red sweat popping on their limbs :

## BOXING DAY

It's a must – a sealed universe

In the back of the shed – marked toys

Instant 1992 – a smell of California

## CHALLENGER CARRIED

1
You – where did you go today
The fields are blank and fallow – gone to mud – tonguing snow
Mountains build themselves for you to climb and to climb
and to unclimb...

2
What sorts of walking occurred on the anniversary of the
Challenger explosion
We – live in water we die in water we are buried in water
If yesterday was a sunny day in January then today must also
be a day...

3
We pass the hospital and the bodega selling flowers at 10pm
The tower in the park looks like an air valve on a tire or swim toy
Releasing – and if Fort Greene were to deflate...

4
The people are dancing again in their living room
All four synchronized – the one in green stares out the window
blankly missing a beat
Practicing a movement for a flashmob that will not...

5
Challenger carried tomato seeds for school children to plant
in Styrofoam cups
The seeds floated in space for 5 years and that – is a peace-filled
thought
Brought back by Colombia – these seeds will not grow...

6
Across the globe we tweet about Egypt
It begins to snow – weightless salt ashes the road
It is 10pm – heads lull – there is deafening silence – and the
internet goes off in Cairo...

## RED OAK

There are three dead spiders in the bottom of the toy box

It is a box covered in contact paper – but is a toy a box a box
    for toys

Ten years it has been stored in this aluminum room
                padlocked from memory :

Toys : unloved    but certainly loved
                a small sapphire ring box
      its almost too small hinge blackened from the darkness :

One fall I collected the caps from acorns : circled them into
      cog wheels   umbrellas in musicals :

It begins to rain : Hold one    then three
place the spider boys in them and set into a puddle-ocean :

How do spiders pick locks :

## RHODODENDRON

The front door of my Mother's parent's house never opens : you enter from the porch in the rear : the driveway leaves you under that great old maple that goes yellow in fall

In the front under the door three great rhododendron whose name means "rose-tree" means "dry" : bursting pink in springtime but thick leafy green and waxy for most of my memory

These plants were considered weeds by settlers too big to see over but short enough to make a mess of twig : hybridization saved them in the hearts and minds of generations

Saved them for this front door where I stand on a cold morning and look into the gray mountains lumping the horizon : the great rhododendron are dying : leaves brittle glowing gold and never pink anymore

Someone tell Thoreau : go draw in the dirt of his grave the words 'rose' 'dry' 'America' : the death of the house of memory : my mother's mother is dead my mother's sister is dead my mother's father is not but my father's mother and father are :

# STUDY (THREE SEASONS)

## I

The nervous system is the figure of a tree
branching – with winter finger tips – reaching for the cloud cover

February is raining gray – the hardest month – raw wool on skin

Your skin settled at rough months ago – the sores in your mouth –

                                        Morphine

More of everything – when you get older you just become
more yourself

These are fingers touching your arm – your asleep-awake

Your eyes are that milky liquid color the ocean goes after storm

There are jellyfish washing up every shore – tentacles melting
into glass

Your death is a bed in a room in a house in Pennsylvania

All bay windows and hissing oxygen

All porch cats and branching Maple trees

The nervous system is the figure of a tree
trembling – Aspen in full golden – you fuzzy-headed woman –

Morphine

February is a sort of slip – a dash –
it is a between month – full of end of winter tired –

It is a moment of sighing at the low full clouds

Each finger desperate wanting –

## 2

The nervous system is the figure of a tree
        repeated below ground – it is a mirror object –
      that spreads in all directions
            it needles into every thing

November is smoothing brown – the dangerous month –
      worm casings

You were only shrinking until one day you were just –

                                Morphine

More of everything – if you never get older do you stay in one
      form

These are your hands – plastic clutching mannequin hands

Cross and beads at your feet – you shine like polished floors

The kind you bare foot on the kind you sock-slide on

Your death is a bed in a room in a house in Pennsylvania

All flower beds and tomatoes

All empty basements filling with cookies

The nervous system is the figure of a tree

        knotting – twisting Cherry – you fuzzy-headed
        woman –

                          Morphine

November is a sort of comma –
    a sitting on a bus – a standing in a museum –

A moment of promises never come – rooms – full and empty

Doors polished into reflecting pools –

# 3

The nervous system is the figure of a tree
feathered and dropping then rebuilding itself

January is a purple bruise – the coldest month – a diamond mistaken for ice

You were pale and falling into a hole that you were filling up –

                                    Morphine

More of everything – you get so old that you become pure self

This is your skin – loose – eyes are drifts of worry

Darting like schools of fish like swallows diving

Death drop – fly until the oxygen is so thin then fold your wings to your chest –

Your death is a bed in a room in a house in Pennsylvania

All magazine clippings

All silent dark hospital rooms with little views of fields and first snows

The nervous system is the figure of a tree
crumbling – unblooming Lilac – you fuzzy-headed woman –

Morphine

January is a full stop
a wrap everything up and hold it – hold it – hold it month

A moment of hardening – sap freezing into copper
holding – all of that energy holding – wait – wait –

That great release of spring –

## HIGHBUSH BLUEBERRY

Is it the taste of open ?

        The space between fingers ?

# HISTORY LESSONS : SANTA FE

7000 feet above sea level a continental rift at the base of the Sangre de Cristo the smallest toe of the Rocky Mountains burn red at sunset burn yellow in autumn and quiver violently with the fingertips of several thousand Aspen.

These foothills are a toe dipping into the flat ocean of New Mexico. The Rockies pile to the north like older brothers watching their sister for signs of growing up. She courts over her shoulder to the people who have come and gone in the centuries she has lived.

You were my first boyfriend and freshmen year I would stretch my fingers across the space between us and touch your fingertips while you were sleeping in my bed I would watch you sleep and catch my breath because I couldn't believe you were real.

The city is surrounded by the pueblo, 2000 years old and in ruins. The oldest house in America is on De Vargas Street. Over 800 years old and made of mud. The San Miguel Mission is the oldest church in America, the bell was cast in 1356. Mass is at 5.

Those early people had hearts that race the same way mine does. They must have imagined carving the land into houses, a perfect mirror of the geometric sky.

So much history. After we graduated we moved in together and I would visit friends on campus and feel the concrete blocks staring at me. You don't believe in this place. You are unaffected by histories.

On September 11$^{th}$ 2001 we sat up watching the television all day. The phone lines were jammed and I didn't get through to my mom until late that night. Your parents were in Manhattan. You rocked silently while I made tea.

These things collapsed. My first view of Santa Fe, the attacks on the World Trade Center, reaching at night for your fingers. The days looked the same. That severe blue. The mountains reaching that final feverish green before going yellow at fall.

I held you and you talked about what it would mean to see your city the next time you were there. I couldn't help but think about the slow falling steel and concrete. The bodies with their arms out like children pretending to be pinwheels.

Severe clear and burning. I think of the center being blown out. The light is dazzling and all I remember is that the smoke made everything powdered and foggy. Like a cool fall morning. Like daybreak after forest fire.

## ELIMINATION

Milky cloudy plastic bag in the boy's hand then
overhead

then

down

With the force of breaking ice

The mid-day street hiccups

A woman turns her head
her mouth glazed radiating alarm from her brow

Bag up

The weight catches mid-swing
rushes the boy's head the part
twisted shut begins to spin open –

then

down

Sound of
meat on counter tops at butcher shops
All that white Pollocked with black blood

The boy raises the bag stares into the cloudy surface

Dark red rises within

    It

        moves

The woman bumps into a man
who also watches then up overhead
                        the bag
                        with the thing inside

          then

      down

## A JOKE

Diatomaceous earth looks like flour
        feels like talc – pumice
enticing – soft to leave footprints

Have you ever rubbed talc
into the cracks in your feet – felt that
        odd dryness of fossilized algae

        – Alfred Nobel
invented dynamite with those
lost German oceans –

        All that pent up sun

A bit of Berlin Wall sits on a shelf – a
pink side
        a green side

The streets of New York are covered
        in bones
but you'll never have enough to make a chicken

## AMERICAN CHESTNUT

Children are taking poles from sheds

Spreading sheets under trees

Are shaking loose 'til sore

Their limbs glass with sweat

## LOVE POEM

We went to watch the stars

I could only see the lights of the city – making a dome – a bubble
                                                                          bent inward –

The outer edges –
        shifted – uncomfortably out of focus
The dome – balanced on lamp-posts – leaned –
                                        a drunken klezmer

You say I have a wild imagination – my eyes see things you will not

I blinked
        You told me I dream too strangely for you –

You are tired of my obsession with lights –

The city started walking – with stainless steel legs – little light-feet casting orange circles on the earth –

        I never told you –

                the city was dropping people like clothes –

## FLOWERING DOGWOOD

Little centers – hard ageless peas –
                        and the tumor in your breast
was no bigger – at first – the tumor in your breast was no bigger
at first it was a break in the sky –

Little hands reach down – caress cheeks pat bottoms – these
hands are burning

The bark of the dogwood makes a bitters –

The berries hold a stone that robins carry farwide
which propagate – grow
                        behind so many houses

## PECAN

There's that joke about Washington and Jefferson sharing a pecan with a slave girl that Jefferson is secretly fucking and I just can't.

Why does everything have to acknowledge its history : the pages of books just keep murdering rooms
        a series of blades : rhetoric pressing flesh drawing blood:

How do you survive : hold that nut in your hand awhile and feel that weight : the girl's skin is that color –

In your mouth it will feel cold hard : smooth like plaster : like the sound of a great owl

Washington might even know approve : maybe he and Jefferson talk positions while thinking about nation building : he looks the other way : sees the flat expanse of Virginia wash away towards something he cannot possibly know yet in classrooms across the land he does he is prophetic clean.

## BUCKEYE

A deep black well

cased in brown and white and red and yellow

A truffle

                      A jellied horse's eye

## ANIMA

Put it right

Force the deer to stand

The smell of river banks held fast with mildew

Thickening blood darkening – all that life pooling

You cannot undead a deer

      When you stop the car you think it's asleep – the sun-warm fur velvet like a pillowcase or a suit jacket – but –

                         the maggots
             which are starting up
     in the belly –

have other ideas – humming their little song working at the everything in the four-chambered stomach
                         – two gallons of process

Rigor doesn't stand

Other drivers see you – diorama of insanity – screaming cradling a dead animal in your arms – blood

in your mouth that tastes like blood tastes like

## AMERICAN ELM

Down the row of trees this green fountain turns yellow it turns brown
Girls skip rope :

       I draw chalk monsters on the sidewalk :

Out back a maple tree swing hanging from a large first limb idles :

We ran between apple trees pear trees plum trees dogwood trees every tree
fell to old age high wind lightening
bark beetles Dutch Elm
gardens sheds :

       The girls grew up :

I look at the sidewalk for lingering lines
       they breathe       little broken mouths  "

runrunrunrunrunrunrunrunrunrun       " :

## BLACK LOCUST

Fold yourself – catch water in your leaves

## LUNGFISH

Water blooms inside you : bicycle tires in the lung

I do not know how to swim : When I was younger they tried

I stood on the side of a pool and stared at that mass of masslessness and I fell in

The view from below : bodies stuck in a ceiling some Sistine nightmare : a child reached for a parent : their hands touched –

My mother is Aquarian : violent headaches take her with the slightest barometrics

Someone asks : 'How can you be a Pisces if you can't swim?'

I tell them about fish that can breathe on land octopus that run between shallow pools on the tips of their suckered legs : I joke about an octopus coming to the door asking if you had a moment to hear about their lord and savior cthulhu and no one laughs

I think about ice on Mars : that little rover all alone digging for some long frozen molecules on another world

When it looks up :
    *can* it look up :
        it can send tweets :
            I don't know if it can see the stars :
if it is a watchtower in the darkness : a lighthouse : a telescope macro-ing and micro-ing without understanding…

    But when it does look up : finally
    does it see a swallowing expanse of blue
    a hand reaching for another

## STUDY (BALLOON BOY)

He is trapped in the basket of the balloon
/
He is hiding in a box in the attic with the spiders

Either way he is a cloud in the shape of a boy

A dark nuclear shadow of a person cast on a wall

Without a face his features begin to fade

He is that image of your parents Marty McFly
                      disappearing

Memory is a lead balloon endlessly expanding
                      it seems

When he returns all we can do is inflate in anger

That the cloud suddenly shifts into focus

That it wasn't the fuzzy outline of an animal after all

That it was just a boy in an attic

Memory is a paper balloon
                      folding itself until the seams tear


This              is the red object

and you fill it

        it will give you that

You can make shapes with it

Crumbs

      along a path

to follow back    to the source


.      Let's talk about string :

How tenuous that you could possibly be linked to anything

Yet

Here is this thread and it is linking you to this bouncing absently in the air

And

The orb or your first kiss or that time in Wal-Mart
The thread is that feeling and smell and color of the moment

It is tied to your wrist

But

You only remember that linking string

The orb floating over there in the dust is only a faint light

That drifts always further away...

I am standing in the bookstore and I cannot remember Walt Whitman's name

I scan the shelves his presence becomes a bearded hole fading at the row of bestsellers

      How did I get here?

My palms are sweating and this shirt is suddenly itchy – I am covered in sunburns

I scratch and stare at the Walstonecraft's the Wordsworths's the Waldrop's –
      E. B. White is of little help

I look into Allen Ginsberg's eyes to see if I can see if I can see –

I must have been attached to something.
Must have been led here

I am looking for my sister – on her birthday
A gift really – what pages should she get lost in that I have been lost in

What memory of a book matches my image of her

These spines have nothing to tell me

They fill and fill with my scratched forgetting – I twist –
      and the sacrum screams

I am a skipping record

．
                Expansion is stretching rubber

It peals and whistles

                Imagine that all growth sounds like this

Your childhood sounded like this

                It still sounds like this

．

There he is hiding – seams are holding

And outside the window is that tree that goes red in the fall

The one that pulls the sun – the one
that dropped that limb in the storm
smashed the windows of the car

Those windows were new – you had driven cross-country
a rock popped the windshield like ice deciding spring, now

Spidering for two-thousand miles

The sound lasting milliseconds.

## YELLOW BIRCH

Autumn is a funerary burn

We make another drive to another hospital in another year

Thin white trunks wave yellow lanterns in a hurricane

Lights come on and the woman in the bed is suddenly old

Eyes scan for translucent worry in the ice

The window adds no light her hands never stop moving

First snow falls it reminds of things that cannot be remembered

Everything smells of compressed air

## CRANBERRY

Hold the universe at bay pack it in rose water moist sugar

Here the ball of reality that bends light like no one's business will dry will candy

The tension a yolk melting across your shoulders

Tomorrow we can talk about pills and night terrors and how it will only rot

Peace go with you brother bury it in sand let it grow in darkness turn white as blindness

The heavens will open and hands rain down will touch the land will singe every last atom

Make a broken jam from your thoughts scoop the leftovers from the bowl

The mirror of the universe is eyes imagining themselves into existence

## GEOMETRY OF CASCADING ROOMS

Celery-sliced ends of calla lilies slow drip into a clear glass
They are tied with purple yarn that make impressions on the green

White blooms lean in the direction of a doorway – a room
tries to assemble itself so it can be described

The talon points of flowers slice air – the sex anxiously waits –
looking for bees

Walls arrive – books make mildew and chairs puff themselves
Crystal glasses fill with thick clear alcohol that casts a green
shadow

Purple threads tie themselves into a Persian rug – one is lost –
snags on a desk leg – this makes everything look worn

Calla lilies drip and the bedroom dismantles itself to make shelves

Bedposts are busy rubbing into powder to mix with water for
paper – books begin to bind without their pages

Glass unmakes into sand then turns an hourglass – the sun starts
to invent the abrupt line of fire just below clouds

Out across the world a tuning begins – floorboards upright and
practice treeing – sand remakes glass – breaks into fine shards
and causes a field

Pages fold themselves into leaves – walls become mesas – soil
and rocks invent the moon and stars – behind all the redness

Calla lilies fill the glass then plant themselves at the edge of melting

# RISTRA

1

Take a pepper from the ristra that hangs on the porch in the rain and in the sun and crush it in your sweaty hands like talcum before the uneven bars

It spreads like smashed beetle shell across the tiled floor in summer like a roach in the kitchen before the baby or the cat can get to it

Eggshell porcelain enameled thick as blood drying on cement after the deer is skinned after the zinnias dry and the coal has been burned

The redness absorbs into your skin and the blood will burn in your veins and the roses will bloom uneven this year and the next they will not bloom at all

2

The uneven bars

of barcode

swing calmly

on the cereal box

That sweet old

man on the oatmeal

is suggesting

you have syrup

All these

bubbling pots

smell like wood

ovens and ash

Thick and black

tar over the plate

then tar over

the table

**3**
When the cat escaped was later found dead and bloated by the roadside his mouth unhinged flies poured endlessly from within

**4**
The paintings of the National Gallery collected dust under Manod Mountain during World War II

In the blackness of a mine everything amasses an inward glow

An eye – ink-filled flecks of gold spun in the darkness of a womb butterflies trying to escape a windowless enclosure

Under pressure paint novas and turns to diamonds

The halls will be darkened and only eyes will be left

5

Underneath the window is a patch of rose bushes that have been allowed to overgrow they spindle in the shadows of autumn and the blooms are tired Victorian gowns
allowing themselves to fade worn at the edges they have bruised themselves unlaced and unlaced themselves

The shears gum black with a strange oil you prune obsessively at the taps where eye-buds wink peeling the thickest sections back until the inner wood is bare breaking exposed you are cutting for new growth but these bushes are fucked

6

Now please,

       put the pepper back together

## HISTORY LESSONS : GROUND ZERO

I have nothing to add.
There is nothing to add.
Never could additions be plenty enough.

Here is a hole.
That bleeds & bleeds & bleeds &...
Girders are rising up and life is continuing as always.

Originally, in 1966, things were carried from here and poured into the Hudson by the cart-load until a bank of land rose from the depths and this city can replicate itself further. 8,000 people live there today.

You can see negative space. How does it take ten years to build a skyscraper? How is this healing. My aunt and grandmother and grandmother have all died since then and those pale patches of skin whisper still.

The World Trade Center is a fractal. Zooming, splintering, repeating. On these shores and on others the pieces fall as sharp snows. I'm not political enough to talk about these things on this day or in this town.

From the east side of the Brooklyn Bridge the Statue of Liberty looks away from the city. As the sun sets the Q train catches red light and Verizon logos. I avoided this as long as I could. You are red-faced, tired.

And we sleep side-by-side as the television plays some marathon of shows about make-overs and motorcycles. A gulf opens between us and we may as well be in separate decades.

I wonder aloud over breakfast about how long it will take for the 9/11 memorials to feel like every other memorial to every other thing. How soon it will just feel like history. I think I say that the light outside looks like it did after the towers fell and you just stare like I am an alien.

I am an alien.
Infection.

Not enough something. You are wistful and seem to hold onto the idea of New York before the towers fell as if it were a different place. A place with less construction, death, fear – with more beauty, hope, divinity…

We will descend quietly into ourselves, we will accept the swirl of contradictions.

www.ingramcontent.com/pod-product-compliance
Lightning Source LLC
Chambersburg PA
CBHW020622300426
44113CB00007B/742